MW01201318

God's Answers to Man's Questions

Milk & Meat Series

Over 1450 questions you can answer from
the book of

JOHN

The Gospel to the World

Book 2 of 7

David Brewer

Milk & Meat Series
by David Brewer

Printed in the United States of America

ISBN 978-1-60266-338-1

We want to hear from you. Please send your comments about this book to us in care of dbbrewer2@bellsouth.net. Also, please visit our website www.milk-meat-series.com for more information about this ministry.

www.xulonpress.com

Contents

—⚮—

Forward

—⁓—

This study guide was written to encourage the student to think through each verse of God's amazing word. Read each verse carefully, ask the Lord for wisdom, and answer the questions. His word is powerful and seeps into our innermost being to help us think and respond wisely.

The Scriptures tell us where we came from, how we are to live on earth and what will happen in the future.

This guide can be used as a daily devotional, for a bible study or with a Sunday school class. I also use it as a reference of my personal responses to the word of God.

I based this study on the New International Version English translation of the Bible. My hope is that you will receive a blessing as you study His word that is true and powerful.

David Brewer

In Appreciation

I am eternally grateful to the men who have influenced me during the thirty-five years of my Christian walk.

It would take many pages to acknowledge each individual who has spent time with me and who has been faithful proclaiming the truths of the scriptures.

However, I do wish to express my gratitude to the following:

Mark G. Cambron	Charles C. Ryrie
Jerry Falwell	C.I. Scofield
Bill Gothard	Richard Seymour
Harry A. Ironside	A. Ray Stanford
William MacDonald	Chuck Swindol
J. Vernon McGee	Elmer Towns
Floyd Radabaugh	Richard VanGorden
Chuck Reed	H.L. Willmington
John R. Rice	John F. Woolvord
	Racy B. Zuck

I also want to thank Back to the Bible, Focus on Grace, Moody Press, Nav Press, RBC Ministries and Word of Life.

"And the things you have heard me say in the presence of many witnesses entrust to reliable men who will also be qualified to teach others." II Timothy 2:2

JOHN

Introduction

—m—

John 20:30-31 - "Jesus did many other miraculous signs in the presence of His disciples, which are not recorded in this book. But these are written that you may believe that Jesus is the Christ, the Son of God, and that by believing, you may have life in His name." (NIV)

The book of John was written to show the world that Jesus was and is God and that He came to die for all.

Using the New International Version English translation of the book of John, I compiled approximately 1450 questions to help the Bible student understand God's written word.

All Scripture is God-breathed and is useful for teaching, rebuking, correcting and training in righteousness, so that the man of God may be thoroughly equipped for every good work. – II Timothy 3:16 (NIV)

Above all, you must understand that no prophecy of Scripture came about by the prophet's own interpretation. For prophecy never had its origin in the will of man, but men spoke from God as they were carried along by the Holy Spirit. – II Peter 1:20-21 (NIV)

May the Holy Spirit change your life as you learn and obey His written word.

David Brewer

John 1

Read each verse and answer the questions.

Topics:
The Word Becomes Flesh
John the Baptist
Baptism
The Lamb of God
Disciples Chosen

Note: *The book of John was written at least 50 years after Christ*
            died and arose.

1:1-2   In the beginning, what was?
Note: *The verb "was" means already in existence – not came into*
            existence – the same as in I John 1:1.
            Where was it?
            Who was this?
            Who was with God in the beginning?
            Who was He?

1:3   Who made all things?
            What was made without Him?

1:4   Where was life?
            What was life?

1:5   Where does this light shine?
            What does not understand?

1:6   Who sent John?

1:7   What was John to do? Why?

1:8   What was this statement about John?

13

1:9   Who gives light to all that come into this world?
              What was He doing at this time?

Note: *God has always revealed Himself to man. Here are 5 ways:*
1.   *In this verse - God makes man to be conscience of Him.*
2.   *Psalm 19 –Creation speaks.*
3.   *John 16:8 – The Holy Spirit convicts.*
4.   *Romans 1:20 – His invisible qualities are seen.*
5.   *Acts 1:8 - The church proclaims.*

1:10   What did the world not recognize?
              Where was he?
              How was the world made?

1:11   Who did not receive Him?
              Where did He come?

1:12   What happens to all that do receive Him?

1:13   What kind of a birth do they have?

1:14   Notice the "Word" in verse 1. What happened to Him?
              Who was that "Word" in verse 1?
              What was seen?
              Where did He come from?
              What was the Father full of?

Note: *Here are other very clear verses to show Jesus was and is*
             God in the flesh: Matthew 1:21 – He was named Jesus,
             meaning God who saves, keeps and defends; Matthew 1:22-
             23, Acts 20:28, Romans 9:5, Hebrews 1:8-9.

1:15   What two things did John teach that were
              contradictory?

1:16   What do we receive because of Him?
              Why?

1:17   Where did the law come from?
             Where did grace and truth come from?
             Who were the first 16 verses speaking about?

Note: *In verse 1, the "Word" was God. In verse 14, the "Word" became flesh. Jesus was and is that "Word."*

1:18   Who made God known?
             Where is He now?
             What is the "One and Only" called here?

1:19-20   What did John testify to?
             Who was he telling this to?

1:21   What questions did they ask John?
             What were his answers?

1:22-23   When they asked who he was, what did he say?
             What prophet did he quote?

1:24-25   What did the Pharisees ask?
             Who were the Pharisees?

Note: *You may need to look in a Bible dictionary.*

1:26-27   *Note: John was dipping people in water, and they were identifying with those that were believers looking for the Messiah. We are baptized, or dipped in water, to identify with the believers that have recognized the Messiah, who is the Lord Jesus Christ that came and paid for all sins, those of both the Old and New Testament believers.*

Notes on Baptism:

"Baptizo" is a Greek word that was placed into the English language. It was not translated. It means to dip, immerse or place into.

Do not use the word water with baptize unless the text warrants. Notice the different kinds of baptisms. If man had anything to do with it, it would be water baptism; if not, it would be Spirit baptism. Spirit baptism means that the Spirit initiates this baptism.

1. **Matthew 3:11 – John's baptism (Water) – Man had a choice.**
    What did John baptize with?
    Why?

John 1:26	*What did John baptize with?*
John 1:31	*Why did he baptize with water?*
John 1:29-34	*Whom was John speaking about? What would He do?*
Acts 19:4	*What reason was given for John's baptism?*
Matthew 3:15	*Why was Jesus baptized with John's baptism?*

2. **Matthew 3:11 – Baptism with the Holy Spirit (Spirit)**

Acts 11:15-16	*What happened? What was remembered?*
I Corinthians 12:12-13	*What are believers baptized into?*

    Who did this?

Romans 6:3-4	*What were they to know? What two baptisms were here?*

    Note: Every believer is placed into the church, which is the body of Christ, and into His death. This is the baptism that saves. This is spirit baptism. There is no water here, and man has nothing to do with this. You believed and then God acted.

3.   *Matthew 3:11 – Baptism of Fire (Spirit)*

    Matthew 3:12   *What is this fire?*
                                    What kind of fire is it?
                                    Whom is it for?

    Note: Those who will not believe will experience this baptism. Man has nothing to do with this. This will be after one rejects Christ and dies. According to the text, this is the Spirit's job.

4.   *I Corinthians 15:29 – Baptism for the dead (Spirit)*
    Note: If the resurrection were not true, we would all be fools to serve. You and I were put into the places of those that served the Lord before we came along. Who will be put into your place (baptized) when you die? This is spirit baptism. The Spirit puts us in places where we are to serve. You have nothing to do with this. You can determine how well you serve, but God the Holy Spirit gives you gifts to serve in place of those that have passed away from their bodies to be with the Lord.

5.   *Matthew 28:18 – Believers Baptism (Water)*

    This is water baptism, which and has been practiced by the church since its beginning in Acts 2. This baptism identifies us with the Lord Jesus Christ and His death for us. It is an outward expression of an inward new birth. As you are baptized (dipped) into the water, you symbolically show that you died with Jesus in judgment and death and arose in a new life. You have something to do with this baptism.

    We know water baptism does not save or pay for our sins because Jesus did that for us – John 1:29.
    We know water baptism does not save because salvation is a gift, not of works – Ephesians 2:8-9.
    We know water baptism does not save because it is not part of the gospel – I Corinthians 1:14-17
    We know water baptism does not save because Jesus did not water baptize anyone – John 4:2

> *We know water baptism does not save because the thief on the cross could not have gone with Jesus to paradise – Luke 23:43.*

6.   *Luke 12:50 – Mark 10:38-39 – Persecution and Death (Physical)*

> *Luke 12:50 –   Who is speaking?*
> *What is the emotion?*
> *What is Jesus speaking about?*

> *Mark 10:38-39 –   This is physical persecution and death. James and John did go through this. Jesus' baptism of death is what saved us. We had nothing to do with this.*

7.   *I Corinthians 10:2 – Baptism into Moses*
> *This phrase was used to unite them together and identify them to Moses and the experience they went through. There was no water here.*

> *Note: The above references are just a few places the word baptize is used. There are hundreds of clear passages that tell us we are saved because of what Jesus did for us. When you find a puzzling verse, do not try to make it interpret the clear verses differently. Let the clear verses help with the unclear.*

> *As you search for truth, you will see that God and His words are true.*

Vernon Locker said it this way:

CHRIST ALONE

> *No works, no merit on my own,*
> *Would I ever dare to plead.*
> *I rest my case on Christ alone,*
> *And that He died for me.*
> *No obedience or faithful fruit,*
> *Will I boast before His throne.*

> *My faith is in the Lamb of God,*
> *I trust in Him alone.*
> *No miracles or wondrous works,*
> *Of mine for sin can pay.*
> *I only plead His precious Blood,*
> *As my One and Only way.*
> *No talents or fine gifts of mine,*
> *Will I hope to help me in.*
> *The only Gift that He'll accept,*
> *Is His Blood for all my sin.*
> *No ordinance or ritual,*
> *Will I add to his Great Cross.*
> *To believe in anyone but CHRIST,*
> *Is to stand condemned and lost.*
> *No trust in my own righteousness,*
> *Or anything in me.*
> *My faith is in His Righteousness,*
> *Given as a GIFT for FREE!*
> *And on that day when home at last,*
> *I'll join the sweet refrain:*
> *All Glory to the lamb of God,*
> *Who for our sins was slain.*

1:28   Where did this all happen? Check your maps.

1:29   The next day, whom did John recognize?
       What would the Lamb do?

Note: *Before Jesus came, sins were atoned for. That means*
          covered. Now they are taken away.

1:30   What did he note for the second time?

1:31   Why did John come baptizing with water?

1:32   What did John testify of?

1:33   How did John recognize Jesus?
          What would He do?

Note: 1. *The Holy Spirit convicts the world. John 16:8.*
           2. *The Holy Spirit seals you the instant you believe. See Ephesians 1:13-14.*
           3. *You were baptized into His body or the church the instant you believed. See I Corinthians 12:13.*
           4. *If you do not have the Holy Spirit, you are not saved. See Romans 8:9.*
           5. *The Holy Spirit is God. See Act 5:3-4.*

1:34   What did John say?

Note: *He was God in verses 1 and 14. In John 5:18, the Jews wanted to kill Him because He was saying that He was God's son, making Himself equal with God. Here are other titles Jesus was given in John:*

1:1	*Word*	*1:34*	*Son of God*
1:1	*God*	*1:41*	*Messiah/ Christ*
1:3	*Creator*	*1:49*	*King of Israel*
1:7	*Light*	*1:51*	*Son of Man*
1:18	*God the One and Only*	*4:42*	*Savior*
1:29	*Lamb of God*	*13:13-14*	*Teacher*
		20:28	*Lord*

1:35-36   What did John say?

1:37   What did John's two disciples do?

1:38-39   What did Jesus ask them?
          What did they ask?
          What did they do?

1:40   Who was Andrew and what did he do?

1:41   What was the first thing he did?
        What did he tell his brother?

1:42   Where did Andrew take his brother?
        What did Jesus know and call him?

1:43   What did Jesus tell Philip?

1:44   Where were these men from? Check your maps.

1:45   What three things did Philip have to say to Nathanael?

1:46   What did Nathanael ask?

1:47   What did Jesus say of Nathanael?
        Could He say that about us?

1:48   What was the question?
        What was Jesus' answer?

1:49   What did Nathanael say of Jesus?

1:50   Why did Nathanael believe?
        What would he soon see?

1:51   What was Nathanael told he would get to see?

Note: *"The Son of God" is Jesus' divine title. "Son of David" was
        His Jewish title, and "Son of Man" is the title that linked
        Him to the earth and man. "Son of God" was used more
        than 80 times.*

Application

1.   What did I learn about our God from this chapter?

2.   Was there a promise for me?

3.   Was there a command for me to obey?

4.   How should this affect my life today?

5.   Summarize this chapter.

John 2

Topics:
Water to Wine
The Temple Cleansed
Resurrection Foretold

2:1   What took place in Cana? Check your map.
                  Who was there?

2:2   Who was invited?

2:3   What did Jesus' mother say?

2:4   What did Jesus say?

Note: *God's time is always on schedule.*

2:5   What did His mother say?

2:6   What was nearby?
                  How large were they?

2:7   What were the servants to do?

2:8   Then what were they told to do?

2:9   Who tasted the wine?
                  What did he not realize?
                  Whom did he call aside?

2:10   What was noticed?
                  What was usually done at weddings?

2:11   What was done here for the first time?
                  What happened because of it?

Note: *Jesus did many miracles but John recorded only 7. He turned water to wine here. He healed an official's son in 4:46-54; He healed an invalid at Bethesda 5:1-9; He fed five thousand 6:1-14; He walked on water 6:15-21; He restored sight 9:1-41; He raised Lazarus from the dead 11:1-44; He filled a net with fish 21:1-15.*

2:12   Where did they go next? Check your map.
Who was with him?

2:13   When did Jesus go to Jerusalem?
Why?

2:14   What did Jesus find in the temple?

2:15   What did Jesus make?
What did Jesus do?

2:16   What did He say?
Whom did He say this to?

2:17   What did the disciples remember?
Where was this written?

2:18   What did the Jews demand?

2:19   What was Jesus' answer?

2:20   What were the Jews thinking?

2:21   What had Jesus referred to?

2:22   Remember that John was writing about what had already happened. What did happen?

2:23   What was happening at the feast and why?

2:24-25   What would Jesus not do?
              Why?
              What did Jesus not need?
              What did He know?

Application

1.   What did I learn about our God from this chapter?

2.   Was there a promise for me?

3.   Was there a command for me to obey?

4.   How should this affect my life today?

5.   Summarize this chapter.

John 3

3:1   Who was Nicodemus?

3:2   When did he come to Jesus?
         What did he say to Jesus?
         What did He realize?

3:3   What was Jesus' reply to him?

Note: *It always helps me to insert "reign" for "kingdom." That is what "kingdom" means. No one can see these truths or God's reign until they are born again.*

3:4   What was Nicodemus thinking?

3:5   What 2 births was Jesus talking about?

3:6   Again, what two births is He talking about?

3:7   What was His emphatic saying?

3:8   What illustration was used?
         What is true about everyone born of the Spirit?

3:9   What question did Nicodemus ask?

3:10   What was Jesus' reply?

3:11   What were the people not doing?

3:12   What did Jesus say He was speaking about?

3:13   *Note: Son of Man was a title that Jesus gave to Himself to show that He was man.*
     What one man came from heaven?

3:14   *Note: In Numbers 21:5-9, Moses put a brass snake on a pole, and those that were bitten had to look at it to be healed. Jesus said He had to be lifted up like that. (crucified)*

3:15   What would people have to do to have eternal life?

3:16   Who loved the world?
     What did He give?
     What must men do to have eternal life?
     What shall not happen if you believe?
Note: *Do you believe?*

3:17   Why did God send His son into this world?

3:18   If you believe, you are not what?
     If you do not believe, what are you already?
     Why is he condemned?

3:19   What is the verdict?

3:20   Who hates light?
     Why do some not come to the light?

3:21   Why do others come to the light?

Note: *Read John 8:12 and write down who the light is.*

3:22   What did they do here?

Note: *In John 4:2, Jesus did not baptize people, but His disciples did.*

3:23   What did John continue to do?
        Why?

3:24   When was this taking place?

3:25   What developed?

3:26   What was John told about Jesus?

3:27   What was his reply?

3:28   What again did John say?

3:29   What illustration was used?
        What joy was now complete for John?

3:30   What must happen?

3:31   Who is above all?
        Whom was John speaking about?
        Where did He come from?

3:32   He testifies, yet what happened?

3:33   He who does accept His words, what does he certify?

3:34   Who speaks the Word of God?
        What does God give without limit?

3:35   What is in the Son's hand?

3:36   What do you have if you believe on the Son?
        What do you have if you do not?

Here are 160 other verses showing that trust in Christ, belief in Christ and faith in Christ are required for us to be saved. They show that salvation from hell is a free gift. What we must do is believe, trust and receive by faith. Believe, trust and receive are synonymous.

Luke

7:48-50	What saved this woman?
7:37	What kind of woman was she?
8:12	What would happen if they believed?
	What causes people not to believe?

John

1:7	Through the light, all men might what?
1:12	What gave you the right to become a child of God?
2:23	What caused many to believe?
	What did they believe on?
3:15	How many that believe in Him will have eternal life?
3:16	Whom did God love?
	What did He give?
	When someone gives you something, is it a gift?
	What 2 things happen if you believe?
3:18	Who is condemned?
	Who is not?
3:36	Whoever believes in Jesus has what?
	Whoever does not believe in Jesus has what?
4:39	Why did many believe?
4:41	Why did many believe here?
4:42	What did they believe here?
5:24	What must you hear to believe?
	What do the believers have?
	What will not happen?
	Why?
5:45-47	Who will be these men's accuser?
	If they would have believed Moses, they would have believed Jesus. Why?
6:29	What is the work of God?
6:35	What promises are for the believer?
6:40	What is God the Father's will?
	What else is promised?
6:47	What truth is given?
7:38	What would happen if they believed?

7:39	What did He mean?
8:24	What happens to those that will not believe that Jesus is God who came to pay for all sin?
8:29-30	What did many do?
8:31-32	When you believe and hold to His teaching, what are you? What happens?
9:35	What question did Jesus ask?
9:36	What did the man say?
9:37	What was Jesus' answer?
9:38	What did the man do?
10:24	What question did the Jews have?
10:25	What did the miracles say? What did they not do?
10:26	Why did they not believe?
10:27	What do His sheep do?
10:28	What does He give to those that believe? Where are they?
10:29	Who is greatest?
10:30	Where are they? Remember, you are in their grip.
11:15	Why was Jesus glad He was not there at the death of Lazarus?
11:25	If you are a believer and the body dies, what happens?
11:26	What is the promise here?
11:41-42	Why did Jesus say what he said?
12:36	What did He say here?
12:46	One who believes is out of what?
13:19	What was He telling them and why?
14:1-6	What will keep your heart from being troubled? Comment on the other verses.
17:20	Whom was He praying for?
17:21	What did He want the world to do?
19:35	The testimony was given. Why?
20:29	Who are blessed?
20:30-31	Why was this all written down?

Acts

3:16	What healed the man?
4:4	When the message was heard, what happened?
4:32	Who was in one accord?
8:12	What happened here?
8:37	What was He to do before He got water baptized?

9:42	*What did many people do here?*
10:43	*What did the prophets testify about?*
10:45	*What kind of men were they?*
11:17	*What happened to the Gentiles that believed?*
11:21	*What happened here and why?*
13:12	*What did the proconsul do? Why?*
13:39	*What brings justification? (declaring a person righteous)*
14:1	*What happened here?*
14:23	*What had these men put their trust in?*
14:27	*The door of what was open to the Gentiles?*
15:7	*What did God do with Peter?*
	What happened?
15:9	*How does God purify hearts?*
16:30-31	*What does this clear message say?*
17:11-12	*When they searched the Scriptures, what happened?*
18:8	*What happened here?*
	What did they do after they believed?
18:27	*Whom was Apollos a great help to?*
20:21	*What was Paul's message?*
26:18	*How are we sanctified?*

Romans

1:16	*The gospel is the power of salvation for whom?*
1:17	*How is righteousness revealed?*
	How does it come to us?
	How should we live?
3:22	*How does this righteousness come?*
	Whom does it come from?
3:23	*How many fall short of the glory of God?*
3:24	*How are we justified here?*
3:25	*Comment on "through faith in His blood."*
3:26	*Why did He do this?*
	What is He to those that have faith in Him?
3:27	*Where is boasting?*
3:28	*What is observed?*
3:30	*There is only one God that can justify. How does he choose to do this?*
4:3	*What does the scripture say about Abraham?*
4:5	*What do faith and trust and work tell us here?*
4:9	*What has the writer been saying about Abraham's faith?*
4:11	*What was circumcision?*

4:13-16	*Read and write observations.*
4:23-25	*Read and write observations.*
5:1	*How have we been justified?*
5:2	*What gained us access into the grace where we stand?*
9:30	*How do we Gentiles obtain righteousness?*
9:31	*Why did Israel not obtain righteousness?*
9:32	*How did they try to obtain righteousness?*
10:4	*What was the end of the law?*
	What is for everyone that believes?
10:6-8	*Read and write observations.*
10:9	*What must be done to be saved?*
10:10	*What happens when the real inner man believes?*
	What else happens?
	Does this mean if you are dumb, you cannot be saved?
10:11	*What does the scripture say?*
11:29-32	*What is irrevocable?*
	What was received and why?
	Are all men, Jew and Gentile, disobedient?
	What does God have for them all?
15:13	*As you trust, what can happen?*

I Corinthians
1:21	*What has God chosen?*

II Corinthians
4:4	*What has Satan done to this world?*

Galatians
2:16	*How are we justified (declared righteous)?*
2:20	*What already took place?*
	How is a believer to live?
	What did Jesus do for us?
3:2	*How did they receive the Holy Spirit?*
3:6	*How has Abraham accredited righteousness?*
3:7	*What were they to understand?*
3:8	*What did the Scripture foretell?*
3:9	*How are we blessed?*
3:11	*Who will be declared righteous by the law?*
	How will we live?
3:14	*What did we receive by faith?*
3:22	*What does this scripture say?*

> How do we receive the promises of God and the promise He gave to Abraham?

3:24   What was the law to do?

> How are we justified (declared righteous)?

3:26   How do we become sons of God?

Ephesians

1:13   How are we marked?

> How did you get this seal?

1:14   What is He called?

1:19   Who has the great power here?

2:8   How were we saved?

> Through what?

> Where is it not from?

> What is it?

Philippians

1:29   What two things were granted to these believers?

3:9   Righteousness that comes from God is by what?

I Thessalonians

2:13   How did these people receive the Word of God?

> Where does this word work now?

4:14   What did they believe?

> What about those fallen asleep?

II Thessalonians

1:10   When Christ comes to be glorified, who will be there?

2:12   Who will be condemned?

2:13   How did God choose for us to be sanctified and saved?

3:2   Who are the wicked and evil?

I Timothy

1:15   Thirty years after Paul was saved, what did he consider himself to be?

1:16   Why was he shown mercy?

3:16   Read the mystery of Godliness. Truly it is greater than all my sins.

4:10   Who is the Savior for all men?

> What must be done to make Him yours?

II Timothy

1:12	*What was Paul convinced of and why?*
1:13	*How were they to keep what they heard?*

Hebrews

4:2	*Why is the gospel of no value to some?*
4:3	*Who can enter His rest?*
6:12	*How do we inherit what is promised?*
10:39	*What are we?*
11:6-7	*How do we please God?*
	How did Noah become heir of righteousness?

I Peter

1:5	*How does faith shield us?*
2:6-7	*What does the scripture say?*
	Whom is He precious to?

I John

5:1	*Who is born of God?*
5:4-5	*Who overcomes the world?*
5:9	*Whose testimony is greatest? Why?*
5:10	*What do non-believers do?*
5:13	*Whom was this written to?*
	Why?

Application

1.   What did I learn about our God from this chapter?

2.   Was there a promise for me?

3.   Was there a command for me to obey?

4.   How should this affect my life today?

5.   Summarize this chapter.

John 4

Topics:
Samaritan Woman Saved
Samaritan Woman Witnesses
A Son Healed
Many Believe

4:1   What did the Pharisees hear?

4:2   Who was really baptizing?

4:3   Where did Jesus go back to? Check your maps.

4:4   Where did He pass through?

4:5   Where did He come to?

4:6   Where did He sit and why?

4:7   Who was at the well?
        What question did He ask?

4:8   Where were His disciples?

4:9   Why did this woman think it strange He would ask her
        for water?

4:10   What would He give if people would ask for it?

4:11   What did she say?

4:12   Who gave this well to the Samaritans?

4:13   What did Jesus say about the water in the well?

4:14	What did He say about the water He had to offer?
	What would this water do?
	What would this person have?
4:15	What did she ask for?
4:16	What did Jesus tell her to do?
4:17-18	What was her answer?
	What else did Jesus tell her about herself?
4:19	What could she see about Jesus?
4:20	What did the Jews claim?
4:21	What did Jesus say was coming?
4:22	What did the Samaritans worship?
	What did the Jews worship?
4:23	What was going to happen?
	What does the Father seek?
4:24	How do true worshipers worship?
4:25	Whom was the Samaritan looking for?
	What would He do when He came?
4:26	Who did Jesus say He was?
4:27	What did the disciples want to ask?
4:28	What did the woman do?
4:29	What did she say?

4:30   What did they do?

4:31   What did the disciples urge?

4:32   What did Jesus say?

4:33   What did the disciples think?

4:34   What was Jesus' food?
        What do we thrive on?

4:35   What was his illustration?

4:36   What was now?
        What should we be rejoicing in?

4:37   What saying is true?
        What was great about this?

4:38   What did He send them to do?

4:39   Why did many believe?
        Are we testifying?

4:40   What did the Samaritan want?

4:41   What continued to happen and why?

4:42   Of what were these people certain?

4:43-44 Where did Jesus go?
        What did Jesus point out?

4:45   Where had the Galileans met Jesus before?

4:46   What did He do in Cana earlier?
        Who was sick?

4:47   What did the ruler do?

4:48   What did Jesus tell them?

4:49   What was the ruler's plea?

4:50   What did the Lord say?
          What did the man do?

4:51   What did the servants have to say?

4:52-53   What question was asked and what happened?

4:54   What was noted here?

Application

1.   What did I learn about our God from this chapter?

2.   Was there a promise for me?

3.   Was there a command for me to obey?

4.   How should this affect my life today?

5.   Summarize this chapter.

John 5

5:1   Why did Jesus go up to Jerusalem?

5:2   Where were they in this verse?

5:3   How many sick people were there?

5:4   *Note: This was not in some early manuscripts. It is believed this was added as a footnote to explain why the people were there. The NIV did not use it.*

5:5   How long was one an invalid?

5:6   What did Jesus ask?

5:7   Why could he not get into the pool?

5:8   What did Jesus tell him to do?

5:9   How soon was he healed and on what day?

5:10   What did the Jews say?

5:11   What did He tell the Jews?

5:12   What did they want to know?

5:13   What could the man tell them?
        Why?

5:14   Jesus found this man later. What did He tell him?

5:15   What could the man now tell the Jews?

5:16   Because Jesus was doing good on the Sabbath, what did the Jews do?

5:17   What did Jesus say?

5:18   What did the Jews understand Jesus to have said?

5:19   What does a son do?

5:20   What does a loving father do?

5:21   What does the Father do?
        What does the Son do?

5:22   Whom has the Father entrusted judgment?

5:23   How do we honor the Father?

5:24   What was He telling them?
        If you hear Jesus' words and believe, what do you have?
        What will this man not be?
        What do you cross over from and to?

5:25   What truth was He telling them?
        What is the promise?

5:26   Where is life found?

5:27   Why did the father give Jesus authority to judge?

5:28-29 Who will hear His voice?
         What two ways will these be separated?

Note: *There will be two resurrections. Also notice Ephesians 2:8-10 says that one must be created in Christ Jesus to do good works.*

5:30   Why is His judgment just?

5:31   One testimony alone is not what?

5:32-33   Who else testified in Christ's favor?

5:34   Why is he telling these things?

5:35   What was John like?

5:36   Why is Jesus' testimony weightier than John's?

5:37   Who testified concerning Jesus?

5:38   Why did many not believe?

5:39   What did the Scriptures testify of?

5:40   What did they refuse?
If they would have come to Him, what would they have had?

5:41   What did He not accept from men?

5:42   What did they not have in their hearts?
Who can read hearts?

5:43   What would they do and not do?

5:44   What did they make no effort to do?
What do we know about God?

5:45   Who will be the accusers of these Jews?
        What were they trusting in?

5:46   If they had believed Moses, whom would they now
        believe in?
        Why?

5:47   They would not believe what Moses wrote so what
        wouldn't they believe now?

Application

1.   What did I learn about our God from this chapter?

2.   Was there a promise for me?

3.   Was there a command for me to obey?

4.   How should this affect my life today?

5.   Summarize this chapter.

John 6

Topics:
Five Thousand Fed
Jesus Walking on Water
Jesus - the Bread of Life
Mixed Reaction

6:1   Check your maps. When was this?
           Where was this?

Note: *The Sea of Galilee was renamed six times in Bible history.*
           It seemed every political leader renamed it after himself.

6:2   Who was following Christ?
           Why?

6:3   What did Jesus do and with whom?

6:4   What was near?

6:5   What did Jesus see when He looked up?
           What did Jesus say to Philip?

6:6   Why did He ask what He did?

6:7   How much money would it take to feed them all?

6:8   Who spoke up?

6:9   What did he say?
           What did he reason?

6:10   What did he have them do?
           What was in this area?
           How many men were there?

6:11   What did Jesus do next?
What did they now have?

6:12   Who all had enough?
Who did not want things to be wasted?
What did He have them do next?

6:13   What was left over?

6:14   What did the people say?

6:15   What did they want to do next?
Why did Jesus withdraw?

6:16-17   What did the disciples do?
What time of day was it?
Who was not there?

6:18   What happened?

6:19   Three miles out, what did they see?
What was the emotion?

6:20   What did Jesus say?
Why?

Note: *Matthew tells about Peter walking on water in Matthew 14:27-32.*

6:21   What seemed to be another miracle?

6:22   What did the crowd realize the next day?

6:23-24   Where did boats come from?
What did these people do?

6:25 What did they ask when they found him?

6:26 What did He tell them?

6:27 What were they and we to work for?
    What were they and we not to work for?
    What is given?
    By whom?
    Who set His approval on this?

6:28 What question did they ask?

6:29 What was His very clear answer?

6:30 What did they ask?

6:31 What did they say their forefathers had?

6:32 Who gave them this manna?

6:33 Who is the bread now?

6:34 What did they say they wanted?

6:35 What did Jesus say he was?
    What would happen if they came and believed?

6:36 What had He already told them?

6:37 What is the promise?

6:38 Why did Jesus come from heaven?

6:39 What 2 comments express the Father's will?

6:40 What is the Father's will for everyone?

6:41   What were they grumbling about?

6:42   What were they reasoning about?
        What was their question?

6:43   What did Jesus say?

6:44   What 2 facts do we know from this verse?

6:45   Where was this written?
        Who will be taught by God?
        Who comes to the Lord?

6:46   Who has seen the Father?

6:47   What is true?

6:48   What is Jesus?

6:49   What happened to those that ate manna?

6:50   If anyone eats the bread of life (Jesus), what happens?

6:51   What was Jesus?
        Where did He come from?
        What would happen to those that ate of this bread?
        What would He give for the life of the world?

6:52   What was happening among the Jews?
        What were the Jews thinking He was saying?

Note: *Verse 63 makes it clear He is speaking spiritually.*

6:53   What must all do to have life?

6:54   Spiritually speaking, we must take into our being that His body was broken and His blood was shed for us to have what?
What happens at the last day?

6:55   What was real?

6:56   Who remains in Him?

Note: *Just as one eats and drinks in order to have physical life, so it is necessary to appropriate Christ in order to have eternal life.*

6:57   Why did Jesus live as the God man on earth?
Why will we live forever?

6:58   What came down from heaven?
What happened to those that fed on manna?
He who feeds on Jesus will live how long?

6:59   Where was He when He taught this?

6:60   What did the disciples think?
What was their question?

6:61-62   What did Jesus ask them?
What was His other question?
What did Jesus say?

6:63   What does the spirit have?
What counts for nothing?
What kind of words was He speaking here?

6:64   What did Jesus know here?

6:65   No one will come to Jesus unless what happens?

Note: *God is the one who provided salvation. He also convicts the world or no one would be saved.*

6:66   What did many of his followers do?

6:67   What did Jesus ask the 12?

6:68   What did Peter say?
             What did Peter know?

6:69   What did they believe?

6:70-71   Why did He choose Judas along with the others?

Application

1.   What did I learn about our God from this chapter?

2.   Was there a promise for me?

3.   Was there a command for me to obey?

4.   How should this affect my life today?

5.   Summarize this chapter.

John 7

Topics:
Feast of Tabernacles
Teaching from God
Believers
Unbelievers

7:1   Why did Jesus stay around Galilee?

7:2   What was near?

7:3   What did His brothers suggest?
        Why?

7:4   Who did they want Him to show Himself to?

7:5   Who did not believe yet?
        What were His brothers' names? (Matthew 13:55)

7:6   Why didn't He go yet?

7:7   Why does the world hate Him so?

7:8   What did He tell His brothers to do?
        What was Jesus awaiting?

7:9   What did He do?

7:10   What did He do after His brothers went up?

7:11   What were the Jews asking?

7:12   What 2 views were expressed about Jesus?

7:13   Why did the people not speak publicly about Jesus?

7:14   The feast was 6 days. In the middle of the week, what did He do?

7:15   What amazed the Jews?

7:16   Who is the source of His teaching?

7:17   What promise is in this verse?

7:18   What 2 truths are mentioned here?

7:19   What were they not doing?
         What were they trying to do?

7:20   What did the crowd say?

7:21   What astonished them?

7:22   What did they do on the Sabbath?

7:23   What was Jesus' reasoning?

7:24   What were they to do?

7:25-26 What were the people asking?
         What did they think the authorities concluded?

7:27   What were they thinking?

7:28-29 Why did they not really know Jesus?
         What did Jesus know?

7:30   What did they try to do?
         Why did they not succeed?

7:31   What did many in the crowd do?
         What questions did they have?

7:32   What did the priests and Pharisees try to do?

7:33   How long would Jesus be there?
          Where did Jesus say He was going?

7:34   What would happen?

7:35-36   What questions did the Jews have?

7:37   At the last day of the feast, what did Jesus say?

7:38   What did the scripture say?

7:39   What did Jesus mean by verse 38?
          Why had the Spirit not come yet?

7:40   What did some of the people say?

7:41   What did others say?
          What questions did they ask?

7:42   What did they know the scriptures taught?

7:43   Why were the people divided?
          Why are they today?

7:44   What did some want to do?

7:45   What question was asked to the temple guards?

7:46   What was their answer?

7:47-48   What questions did the Pharisees ask?

7:49   Whom did they consider cursed?

7:50   *Note: Nicodemus of Chapter 3*

7:51   What question did he ask?

7:52   What was their reply?

7:53   Where did they all go?

Note: *The earliest manuscripts did not have 7:53-8:11. This omission would not take away from truth. John 20:30 tells us that not everything Jesus did was recorded but only what was needed for people to believe. This probably was true and will be treated as such.*

Application

1.   What did I learn about our God from this chapter?

2.   Was there a promise for me?

3.   Was there a command for me to obey?

4.   How should this affect my life today?

5.   Summarize this chapter.

John 8

Topics:
Forgiveness
The Light of the World
True Words
Abraham's Children
The Devil's Children

8:1   Where did Jesus go?

8:2   Where was He found at dawn?
           Where were all the people?

8:3   What did the Pharisees do?

8:4   What did they say?

8:5   What question did they ask Him?

8:6   Why were they asking these questions?
           What was Jesus doing as they were asking questions?

8:7   What statement did Jesus make?

8:8   What did He do next?

8:9   What did those that heard do?
           Who went away first?

8:10   What 2 questions did Jesus ask the woman?

8:11   What was her answer and His?

8:12   What does Jesus call Himself here?
           What promise is ours?

8:13   What did the Pharisees say?

8:14   Why did Jesus really not need another witness?
What did He know that they did not?

8:15-16   How do men judge?
When He does judge, why are His decisions right?

8:17   What did the law teach?

8:18   What other witnesses did He have beside Himself?

8:19   What question did they ask Him?
If they would have known Jesus, whom else would they have known?

8:20   Where was He speaking?
Why did they not seize Him?

8:21   What did He say to them again?

8:22   What did the Jews ask?

8:23   What contrasts are mentioned here?

8:24   Why would they die in their sins?

8:25   When they asked, "Who are you?" what did Jesus say?

8:26   What is true here?

8:27   What did they not understand?

8:28   After the resurrection, what would they understand?

8:29   What did Jesus always do?

8:30   As He was speaking, what was happening?

8:31   What did He say to the Jews?

8:32   What does the truth do for us?

8:33   What was puzzling them?

8:34   Who is a slave?

8:35   What does a slave not have?
Who is part of the family?

8:36   Who really sets us free?

8:37   Why did they want to kill Him?

8:38   What was Jesus telling them?

8:39   What did they answer?
Why did He think they were not Abraham's children?

8:40   What had Jesus told them?
What would Abraham not do?

8:41   What did Jesus say they were doing?
What did these people claim to be?

8:42   If God were their father, what would they do?
Why?

8:43   What was the question?
What was the answer?

8:44   Who was their real father?
        What do we know about the devil?
        What is the devil a father of?

8:45   He told them the truth, but what was their response?

8:46   What 2 questions did He ask?

8:47   Who can hear?
        Why could they not hear, spiritually speaking?

8:48   What did they accuse Jesus of?

8:49   Whom did Jesus honor and whom did they dishonor?

8:50   Was Jesus seeking glory for Himself?
        Who is it that seeks it?

Note: *When we glorify God, what we do is just make Him known.*
        Just the truth about Him brings Him glory.

8:51   What happens if you keep His word?

8:52   What did they say they knew about Jesus?
        Why?

8:53   What 2 questions did they ask?

8:54   Who glorifies Jesus?

8:55   What did He call these people?
        What did Jesus know that they did not know?

8:56   What did Abraham rejoice in?
        What did he see?

8:57   What confused these Jews?

8:58-59   What was Jesus telling them?
           What did He call Himself?
           What did the Jews then try to do?

Note: *What Jesus was saying here was the same thing His father said in Exodus 3:14. They understood; that is why in verse 59 they wanted to kill Him.*

Application

1.   What did I learn about our God from this chapter?

2.   Was there a promise for me?

3.   Was there a command for me to obey?

4.   How should this affect my life today?

5.   Summarize this chapter.

John 9

Topics:
Blind Man Sees
Pharisees Protest
Spiritual Blindness

9:1   What did He see here?

9:2   What 2 people did the disciples think may have sinned?

9:3   Why was this man born blind?

Note: *All sickness, diseases and physical abnormalities entered
           the human race at the fall in the garden. Human frailty is
           part of the curse. Sometimes we are sick because we pick
           up a germ. Sometimes sickness is permitted to glorify God
           as in John 9:2-3. Sometimes it is because of our sin as in
           I Corinthians 11:30. Sometimes Satan is the problem as
           in Job 2:7. At all times, God our father permits physical
           problems for our good—Romans 8:28. He may heal miracu-
           lously. He may not heal the infirmity. The body may heal
           itself or medicine may be used. Jesus said those who are
           sick need a physician. In James 5:14-15, there appears to
           be sin in this believer's life. God, the perfect father, will
           reveal your sins to you if you do what this verse says and the
           elders do their part. God always does remain faithful. Also
           remember I John 3:14-15.*

9:4   When should we get busy and work?

9:5   What did Jesus call himself?

9:6   What did Jesus do?

9:7   What did He have this man do?
           What miracle was performed?

9:8   What was being asked?

9:9   What did people say?
         What did the man say?

9:10   What did they ask?

9:11   In 4 comments, explain what the man said happened.

9:12   What question was asked?

9:13   What did they do with this man?

9:14   What day did Jesus heal this man?

9:15   What did the Pharisees ask the man?
         What did he say?

9:16   Why were the people divided?

9:17   What question did they ask this man?
         What was his answer?

9:18   Whom did they send for next?

9:19   What 3 questions were asked?

9:20   What could they say?

9:21   What else did they say?

9:22   Why were they afraid?
         What had the Jews already decided?

9:23   Why did they answer the way they did?
         What was their answer?

9:24   What did they tell the man who now had sight?

9:25   What did he know for sure?

9:26   What 2 questions did the Pharisees ask?

9:27   What 2 questions did the man ask?

9:28   What did the Pharisees do?
           Whose disciples did they say they were?

9:29   What did they say about Moses?
           What did they not know about Jesus?

9:30   What was remarkable?

9:31-33   What 3 statements did he use to reason with them?

9:34   What did they say to this man?
           What did they do to him?

9:35   Jesus found the man and what did He ask?

9:36   What did the man ask?

9:37   What did Jesus say?

9:38   What did the man say and do?

9:39   *Note: Jesus came into the world to save sinners; yet because
           of their unbelief, judgment has come also. Many people are
           spiritually deaf and spiritually blind.*

9:40   What did the Pharisees ask Jesus?

9:41   What did Jesus say to them?

Application

1. What did I learn about our God from this chapter?

2. Was there a promise for me?

3. Was there a command for me to obey?

4. How should this affect my life today?

5. Summarize this chapter.

John 10

Topics:
The One Gate
The Good Shepherd
Eternal Security
Jewish Unbelief

10:1   Who is a thief and a robber?

10:2   Who enters by the gate?

10:3   How does He get His sheep out?

10:4   Why do His sheep follow Him?

10:5   Why would they run away from strangers?

10:6   *Note: Jesus was using these stories to teach spiritual truths.*
         John 3:3 teaches people must be born again to understand
         the reign of God or God's kingdom. I Corinthians 2:14-16
         also tells us the lost man cannot understand spiritual truth.

10:7   What is Christ to the sheep?

10:8   Who were they that came before Christ?
         Who would not listen to them?

10:9   What happens to those that come through Christ?
         What will they be able to do?

10:10   What is the motive of the thief?
         Why did Christ come?

10:11   What does a good shepherd do?

10:12   What does the hired hand do?
         Why?

10:13   Why does he run away?

10:14   Who was Jesus?
         What does He know?
         What do His sheep know?

Note: *This is true. Do you know the shepherd?*

10:15   How well do we know Him and He know us?
         What did Jesus do for the sheep?

10:16   The believing Jews were of one sheep pen. Believers
         of the Gentile nation were of a different fold. What was
         He going to do?

10:17   What does Jesus indicate He will do?

10:18   Who really had the power to kill Jesus?
         What authority did Jesus have?

10:19-21 They were divided in their thinking. What were their
         divisions?

10:22   What time of year was it?

10:23   Where was Jesus walking?

10:24   What question did they ask Him?

10:25   What was his answer? Also note 4:26, 8:58

10:26   Why would they not believe?

10:27   What will his sheep do?

10:28   What does Christ give?
          What will never happen?
          What can no man do?
          Where are His sheep found?
          How long is eternal?

10:29   Who is the greatest of all?
          Where are the sheep in this verse?

10:30   Jesus and the Father are what?

10:31   What did the Jews do?

10:32   What did Jesus ask?

10:33   What was clear that they did not like?

10:34-35 *Note: You may want to look these up in a good commentary.*
          When you obey those that God has put over you, you are
          obeying God. These 2 verses were showing them that they
          had no right to stone Jesus. He used an Old Testament verse
          to show that judges were stand-ins for God himself. Jesus
          the God man was God in flesh.

10:36   Why did Jesus tell them they were trying to kill Him?

10:37   When were they not to believe?

10:38   What should the miracles have taught them?

10:39   What did they try to do again?

10:40   Where did Jesus go?

10:41   What did they note about John?

10:42   What happened in this place where Jesus was?

Application

1.   What did I learn about our God from this chapter?

2.   Was there a promise for me?

3.   Was there a command for me to obey?

4.   How should this affect my life today?

5.   Summarize this chapter.

John 11

Topics:
God's Perfect Timing
Jesus - the Resurrection and the Life
Lazarus Arose
Many Believers
Many Doubters

11:1   Who was sick and where did he live? Check your maps.

11:2   Who was this man's sister?

11:3   What message did they send Jesus?

11:4   What did He say was the reason for this sickness?

11:5   What is noted about these people?

11:6   How long did Jesus stay put?

11:7   Then what did He say?

11:8   What did the disciples say?

11:9-10   Think on these verses, commenting if you so choose.

11:11   *Note: The Scriptures used sleep as a metaphor for the death of believers. Mark 5:39, Acts 7:60, I Thessalonians 4:13*

11:12   What did they say?

11:13   What is cleared up here?

11:14   What did He say plainly?

11:15   Why was He glad He was not there when Lazarus died?

11:16   What did Thomas say?

11:17   What did they find when they got to Bethany?

11:18   How far was Bethany from Jerusalem?

11:19   Who was there and why?

11:20   What did Martha do?
        What did Mary do?

11:21   What did she tell Jesus?

11:22   What did she know?

11:23   What did Jesus say to her?

11:24   What did Martha know?

11:25   What is Jesus and what is His promise?

11:26   What truth can we as believers claim?
        What did He ask Martha?

11:27   What was Martha's response?
        Can you say this?

11:28   What did Martha do next?
        Who was asking for Mary?

11:29   What did Mary do?

11:30   Where was Jesus?

11:31   Who followed Mary and why?

11:32   What did Mary say?

11:33   What did Jesus notice?
            Where was Jesus moved and troubled?

11:34   What did He ask?
            What was their reply?

11:35   What did He do?

11:36   What did the Jews think?

11:37   What statement was made?

11:38   What was Jesus' emotion?
            Where did they go?
            What did this tomb resemble?

11:39   What did Jesus say and what did Martha say?
            Why would there be a bad odor?

11:40   What did He promise?

11:41   What did they do and what did Jesus say?

11:42   Why did He speak aloud?
            What can every believer know?

11:43   What words did Jesus call out?

11:44   Who came out?
            How was he wrapped?
            Note: Jesus was also wrapped after His birth.

11:45	What happened? Why?
11:46	What did others do?
11:47	What was called? What was the question? What was Jesus doing?
11:48	What worried them?
11:49	Who spoke up? What were his words?
11:50	What was he saying?
Note:	*Discuss this statement more. I am sure it has a great prophecy of the substitutionary payment of Jesus. Also in verses 51 and 52, we find it was Jesus who would die for all children of God and unite them together (the Church).*
11:51	What did he prophesy?
11:52	What else was prophesied?
11:53	From that day on, what did they plan?
11:54	What did Jesus do?
11:55	What were the people doing? Why?

11:56-57   What was happening?
             What did they want to know?
             Where were they?
             What order was given?

Application

1.   What did I learn about our God from this chapter?

2.   Was there a promise for me?

3.   Was there a command for me to obey?

4.   How should this affect my life today?

5.   Summarize this chapter.

John 12

Topics:
Jesus Anointed for Death
The King's Arrival
Resurrection Predicted
Hearts Hardened

12:1   Six days before the Passover, where did Jesus arrive?
        Who lived there?

12:2   In whose honor was a dinner held?
        Who was serving?

12:3   What did Mary do?
        What filled the house?
        How did she wipe His feet?

12:4   Who objected?
        What would he eventually do?

12:5   What question was asked?
        How much was it worth?

12:6   Why did he really object?

12:7   What did Jesus say?
        What was this perfume for?

12:8   What will we always have among us?

12:9   What did the large crowd want to see?

12:10   Who did the chief priests want dead?

12:11   Why?

12:12   The next day, what did the crowd hear?
         Why were they there?

12:13   What were they doing and shouting?
         Who did they realize he was?

12:14   What did Jesus do?

12:15   What was written?
         Where?

12:16   What did they find out after His death and resurrection?

12:17   What was the crowd doing?

12:18   How many came?
         Why did they come?

12:19   What were the Pharisees upset about?

12:20-21 To whom did they speak?
         What was their question?

12:22   Who told Jesus?

12:23   What had finally come?

12:24   If grain dies and falls to the ground, what happens?

12:25   Discuss this saying.

12:26   What must we do to serve Christ?
         Where will the servant be?
         Whom will the Father honor?

12:27	What was troubled? Why wouldn't He say, "Father, save me from this hour"?
12:28	What was Jesus' request? What did the voice from heaven say?
12:29	What did the crowd say? Why?
12:30	What was the purpose of the voice?
12:31	What was it time for?
12:32	What would He do when He was resurrected? How many men would He draw to himself?
12:33	Why did He say what He said?
12:34	What did they know from the law? What was their question?
12:35	Discuss this comment.
12:36	What did Jesus tell them to do? What did He do?
12:37	Even though many saw the signs, what would they not do?
12:38	What prophet was quoted?
12:39-40	Isaiah gave a reason many would not believe. What was it?

12:41   What did Isaiah see?
        Who was Isaiah speaking about?

12:42   What do we see here?
        How about you?
        Is it possible to be a believer and desire praise from
        men more than praise from God?
Note: *This is called the old nature.*

12:43   What can happen to all of us?

12:44   What must we believe in if we believe in Jesus?

12:45   When they saw Jesus, whom else did they see?

12:46   Why did Jesus come into the world?
        When you believe, what will happen?

12:47   What was His main purpose for coming into the world?

12:48   What will eventually condemn?

12:49   Why did Jesus say what He said?

12:50   Where do His words lead?

Application

1.   What did I learn about our God from this chapter?

2.   Was there a promise for me?

3.   Was there a command for me to obey?

4.   How should this affect my life today?

5.   Summarize this chapter.

John 13

Topics:
Example of Humility
Betrayal Foretold
Death Foretold
Denial Foretold

13:1   What time of year was this?
Jesus knowing what was about to happen was going to
show what?

13:2   What was being served?
What had the devil already done?

13:3   What 3 things did Jesus know?

13:4   What did He do?

13:5   What next?

13:6   What question did Peter have?

13:7   What did the Lord say?

13:8   What did Peter say?
What was the Lord's response?

13:9   What did Peter then say?

13:10-11 *Note: When you are cleansed (saved), you do not need to
take another bath (be saved again). But you might need to
wash your feet when they get dirty. We are saved or cleansed
when we put our faith in Christ, yet we need to daily confess
our sins (I John 1:9). He also noted one that was not clean,
Judas Iscariot.*

13:12   What question did Jesus ask?

13:13   What did they rightly call Him?

13:14-15 What example should we follow?

13:16-17 *Note: Our Lord humbled himself for us. We should do like-wise for others.*
What is the promise?

13:18   Another scripture is being fulfilled about whom?
Where was this prophesied?

13:19   Why did He tell them ahead of time?

13:20   When people accepted Jesus, they were accepting whom?
When people accepted those whom Jesus sent, whom were they accepting?

13:21   Where was Jesus troubled?
What did He now tell them?

13:22   What did the disciples do?

13:23   Who was next to Jesus?

13:24   What did Peter say to Him?

13:25   What question did He ask?

13:26   Who was it? Note verse 18.

13:27   What did Jesus tell him?

13:28   Who understood what Jesus said?

13:29   What did they think He told Judas to do?

13:30   What did Judas do?

13:31-32 Who was going to be glorified?

13:33   What did He tell the Jews that He was telling His disciples?

13:34   What new command was given?

13:35   How will people know if we are Jesus' disciples?

13:36   What was Jesus' reply to Peter's question?

13:37   What did Peter ask and say?

13:38   What did Jesus say Peter would do?

Application

1.   What did I learn about our God from this chapter?

2.   Was there a promise for me?

3.   Was there a command for me to obey?

4.   How should this affect my life today?

5.   Summarize this chapter.

John 14

Topics:
Heaven's Reality
Jesus - The Only Way
The Holy Spirit's Coming
Obedient Love
Peace

14:1   What were they to do to keep from being troubled?

14:2   Where was He going to prepare a place for us?

14:3   What was the promise?

14:4   What did Jesus say they knew?

14:5   What question did Thomas ask?

14:6   What 3 things did Jesus say He is?
            What is the only way to come to God?

14:7   How can we know the Father?

14:8   What did Philip ask of his Lord?

14:9   What question did Jesus ask Philip?

14:10   What did Jesus ask?
            Who is in Jesus?
            What was the Father doing?

14:11   If that was hard to believe, what evidence was given?

14:12   Those who have faith could do what?
         Why? (Saving souls is greater than healing bodies.)

14:13-14 Why would Jesus do what we ask?

Note: Live in the center of God's will; walk in fellowship with the Lord. Ask for anything that the Lord would desire and your prayers will be answered.

Five reasons prayer may not be answered:
1. Unconfessed sin – Psalm 66:18-20
2. Unbelief – James 1:6-7
3. Neglecting the word of God – Proverbs 28:9
4. No fellowship between husband and wife – I Peter 3:7
5. No mercy – Proverbs 21:13

Three ways God answers prayer: Yes, No, Wait. All 3 are answered prayer.

14:15   How do you show love to Jesus?

14:16   What was this promise?

14:17   Why does the world not accept this truth?

14:18   What 2 promises are given?

14:19   What 3 promises are here?

14:20   Where is Christ? Where are we?

14:21   How can you express love to Jesus?
         Who does the Father express His love to?
         What will Jesus do to those that love Him?

14:22   *Note: Notice again John 3:3. Why do we see so many things that the world does not?*

14:23   How do you show love to Christ?
         Why is God at home with people?

14:24   Why do some not obey His teaching?
Note: *I Corinthians 13:4-7. Love is an action, not a feeling.*
         Those who love Him will take action.
         Whose words are these?

14:25   What did Jesus do while He was here?

14:26   What will the Holy Spirit do when He comes?

14:27   What would Jesus give when He left?
         What 2 things are we not to do?

14:28   What had they already heard Him say?
         Why should they have been glad Jesus left?

14:29   Why did He tell them beforehand what He would do?

14:30   Who was coming?
         Who did he not have hold of?

14:31   What must the world learn?

Application

1.   What did I learn about our God from this chapter?

2.   Was there a promise for me?

3.   Was there a command for me to obey?

4.   How should this affect my life today?

5.   Summarize this chapter.

John 15

Topics:
The True Vine
Fruitfulness
Hatred of the World

Note: *Here is another of the "I Am's" found in John. This is*
             not teaching about salvation but about "fruit bearing."
             Ephesians 2:8-9 is very clear. Salvation is a gift of God
             through faith, but fruit is what takes place when we obey
             God's word.

             I John 3:24 says, "Those who obey His command live in
             (abide in) Him." To be saved is one thing. To obey His word
             is another. Obeying His word brings fruit.

15:1   What is Christ here?
          What kind of vine?
          Who is the gardener?

15:2   What does the gardener do to those branches that bear
          no fruit?
          Why does he prune branches?

15:3   How were these disciples already cleaned?

15:4   What needs to be done to bear fruit?

15:5   Who is the vine that helps us to be fruitful?
          Who are the branches?
          If you abide or remain in Him, what happens?
          If you do not, what happens?

15:6   What are we like if we do not abide and remain in Him?

I Cor. 3:11-15	What happens if we are not fruitful?
15:7	What 2 things are needed to have our requests granted?
15:8	What is to the glory of God? What shows we are disciples of Christ?
15:9-10	How do we remain, or abide, in His love?
15:11	Why do we need to know these things about fruit bearing?
15:12	What command is given here?
15:13	What is the greatest love?
15:14	What makes us Jesus' friend?
15:15	Why does He not call us servants?
15:16	Why did Jesus choose these men?
15:17	Again, what was His command?
15:18	If the world hated them, what were they to remember?
15:19	What does the world love? What has the Lord chosen for the believers?
15:20	What 3 truths did He proclaim here?
15:21	Why will they treat them and us that way?
15:22	What excuse does the world have for sin?

15:23	Those that hate Jesus, also hate whom else?
15:24	What did Jesus do in the world that no one else could do?
15:25	Why did they hate Him?
15:26	When the Counselor (the Holy Spirit) comes, and He did, about whom was He to testify?
15:27	Who else was to testify?

Application

1. What did I learn about our God from this chapter?

2. Was there a promise for me?

3. Was there a command for me to obey?

4. How should this affect my life today?

5. Summarize this chapter.

John 16

Topics:
The Holy Spirit's working
Grief to Joy
Belief and Assurance

16:1   Why did He teach all of this?

16:2   What was foretold about these men?
            What would these killers believe?

16:3   Why would the world do such things?

16:4   Why did He tell them this now instead of earlier?
            What was the purpose for telling them?

16:5-6   Where was He going?
            Why did they not ask where He was going?

16:7   Why was He going?
            Whom would He send?

16:8   What would this one do when He comes?

Note: *He does this today.*

16:9   What was the sin?

16:10-11   *Note: The fact that He was going back to heaven proved all*
            things He said were right, and Satan is now condemned.

16:12   What did Jesus have to say?
            Why did He not say them?

16:13   What would the Holy Spirit do when He came?
What would He speak?
What would He tell?

16:14   How was He going to bring glory to Christ?

16:15   Why did He say these things about the Spirit?

Note: *After the Spirit came, He revealed all about the church and the future. This is found throughout the New Testament.*

16:16   What did this foretell?

16:17   What did the disciples ask?

16:18   What other questions were they asking themselves?
At that time, what did they understand?

16:19   What did Jesus notice?

16:20   What did He say they would do while the world rejoices?
Then what would happen?

16:21   What illustration would express the next few days of their life?

16:22   What would happen?
What is the promise about joy?

16:23   What did He promise the Father would give them?

16:24   What had they not done?
What were the promises?

Note: *The disciples were given all the answers to the things they did not understand after the resurrection and after the Holy Spirit came.*

16:25   How was He speaking to them?
          What would happen soon?

16:26   *Note: From the time of the resurrection, we ask the Father*
          in Jesus' name. We go right to the Father.

16:27   Why has the Father loved us personally?

16:28   Where did Jesus come from and where was He going?

16:29   What did the disciples say now?

16:30   *Note: They did not need to ask questions; it was clear. He*
          came from God. God is the Trinity, and they now understood
          Jesus is God the Son.

16:31   What did Jesus say?

16:32   What was predicted next?

16:33   Where is peace found?
          Where is trouble found?
          What has Jesus done?

Application

1.   What did I learn about our God from this chapter?

2.   Was there a promise for me?

3.   Was there a command for me to obey?

4.   How should this affect my life today?

5.   Summarize this chapter.

John 17

Topics:
Jesus' Prayer for Himself
Jesus' Prayer for His Disciples
Jesus' Prayer for Us

17:1   After He spoke those words to the disciples, what did He do?
What did He ask?

17:2   What did God grant the Son?
Why?

17:3   What is eternal life?

17:4   How did Jesus bring God the Father glory?

17:5   What did He ask?
Where did Jesus have this glory before?

17:6   Whom did Jesus reveal?
Who did he reveal to?
What did they do?

17:7   What did the disciples understand and know at that time?

17:8   What did He give them?
What did they, the disciples, do with them?
What did they know for certain?

17:9   Who was He praying for?

Note: *He did pray for the world at other times. On the cross, He prayed that the Father would forgive them for they knew not what they were doing.*

17:10   What belongs to whom?
         How did Jesus get more glory?

17:11   What did He ask the Father to do?

17:12   How were they protected while they were here?
         Who was doomed for destruction?
         Why?

17:13   Why was He praying at that time?

17:14   Why were they hated?

17:15   What was He praying for here?

17:16   *Note: Believers are not at home in this world. Our home is
         in heaven.*

17:17   What is truth?
         What does truth do?

Note: *Sanctify means set apart for God and His holy purposes.*

17:18   Where were they sent?

17:19   Why did Jesus sanctify (set apart) himself?

17:20   Who was Jesus praying for here?

17:21   What 2 things did He want for us?

17:22   How did He want us united?

17:23   What should we let the world know?

17:24   What did He want the believers to see?

17:25   What did the disciples know that the world did not know?

17:26   What did He do for us, and what will He continue to do?
          Why?
          Where is Jesus now?

Application

1.   What did I learn about our God from this chapter?

2.   Was there a promise for me?

3.   Was there a command for me to obey?

4.   How should this affect my life today?

5.   Summarize this chapter.

John 18

Topics:
The Arrest
Peter's Denial
No Fault Found

18:1	Where did He go after the prayer?
18:2	What did Judas know?
18:3	Whom did Judas bring to the grove? What were they carrying?
18:4	What did Jesus know? What did He ask?
18:5	When they told Jesus whom they wanted, what did He say?
18:6	What happened when Jesus told them, "I am he"?
18:7	What did Jesus ask them after they got up? What was their answer?
18:8	What did He tell them to do with His disciples?
18:9	Why?
18:10	What did Peter do? What was the servant's name?
Luke 22:51	What did Jesus do with the ear?
18:11	What was Jesus' command? Why?

18:12   Who arrested Jesus?
        What did they do to Him?

18:13   Who did they take Jesus to?
        Who was he?

18:14   What did Caiaphas recommend?

18:15   Where did Peter and another disciple go?
        How could Peter do this?

18:16   Why did Peter stay outside but later was admitted?

18:17   What was Peter asked that he denied?

18:18   What were they doing and why?

18:19   What information were they seeking from Jesus?

18:20   What did Jesus reply?
        What did He do in secret?

18:21   Whom did He tell them to ask to be witnesses?

18:22   What did they do to Jesus?
        What question did they ask Jesus?

18:23   What was His reply?

18:24   Where did they take Him next?

18:25   What did someone ask Peter again that he denied?

18:26   Who challenged Peter?
        What did he ask Peter?

18:27   What did Peter do again?
         What happened at that moment?

Note: *John 13:38 – This was foretold.*

18:28   Where did they go next?
         What time was it?
         Why did they not go inside?

18:29   What did Pilate do and then ask?

18:30   What was their reply?

Note: *They had no charges.*

18:31   What did Pilate tell the Jews?
         Why did the Jews object?

18:32   Why did this happen?

Note: *Romans were the only ones that crucified people and this method of execution was foretold in the Old Testament about Jesus.*

18:33   Pilate went inside and asked them to bring Jesus in.
         What did he ask Jesus?

18:34   What did Jesus ask Pilate?

18:35   What did Pilate ask Jesus?

18:36   What did Jesus say about His kingdom?

18:37   What did Pilate state?
         What was Jesus' clear answer?
         Why did Jesus say He was born?
         Those on the side of truth do what?

18:38   What did Pilate ask?
         What did he find against Jesus?

18:39   What was the custom?
         What did he ask the Jews?

18:40   What did they shout?
         Whom did they want released?

Application

1.   What did I learn about our God from this chapter?

2.   Was there a promise for me?

3.   Was there a command for me to obey?

4.   How should this affect my life today?

5.   Summarize this chapter.

John 19

Topics:
Jesus Beaten
The King Rejected
Jesus Crucified
Jesus' Death
Jesus Buried

19:1   What did Pilate do to Jesus?

19:2-3   What 4 things did the soldiers do?

19:4   What did Pilate say?
          What could he not find?

19:5   What was Jesus wearing?
          What was Pilate's sarcastic remark?

19:6   What did they say when He came out?
          What did Pilate again say?

19:7   Why did the Jews say they wanted to kill Him?

19:8   What did Pilate hear that caused him fear?

19:9   What did Pilate ask Jesus next?
          What was the answer?

19:10   What 2 questions did Pilate ask next?
          What did Pilate think he had?

19:11   Where did Pilate get his power?
          Who was guilty of a greater sin?

19:12   Pilate wanted to set Jesus free but what happened?

19:13   Where did Pilate sit?
          What was it called?

19:14   What day and hour was it?
          What did he say to the Jews?

19:15   What did they shout?
          What did Pilate ask?
          What did the Chief Priest answer?

19:16   What did Pilate finally do?
          Who took charge?

19:17   What did Jesus carry?
          To where?

19:18   What did they do to Him?
          Who else was crucified?

19:19   What did the notice on the cross say?

19:20   In what 3 languages was the sign written?

19:21   What did the chief priest request?

19:22   What was Pilate's answer?

19:23   What did the soldiers do?
          Describe the piece that was left?`

19:24   What did they do that was foretold?

19:25   Who was near the cross?

19:26   What did Jesus say to His mother?

19:27   Who took care of Jesus' mother?

19:28   What did Jesus say to fulfill scripture?

19:29   What was done next?

19:30   What did Jesus say?
         What did He do?

19:31   What day was it?
         What was the next day?
         Why did they want Jesus' legs broken?

19:32   What did the soldiers do?

19:33   Why did they not break Jesus' legs?

19:34   What did they do to him?

19:35   Why was this testimony given?

19:36-37 What 2 things were foretold?

19:38   Who was Joseph?
         Why was he secretly a disciple?

19:39   Who was with him?

19:40   What was done with the body and why?

19:41   What was there where Jesus was crucified?
         What was in the garden?

19:42   Why did they put His body there?

Application

1.   What did I learn about our God from this chapter?

2.   Was there a promise for me?

3.   Was there a command for me to obey?

4.   How should this affect my life today?

5.   Summarize this chapter.

John 20

Topics:
The Risen Lord
The Lord's Appearance
Rejoicing
Blessings

20:1   When did Mary Magdalene come to the tomb?
              What did she find?

20:2   Whom did she find?
              What was her proclamation?

20:3   What did these disciples do?

20:4   Who was the fastest runner?

Note: *Throughout this book, John refers to himself but never writes his name.*

20:5   Where did he stop?
              What did he see?

20:6   What did he see?
              Who went into the tomb?

20:7   What else is noted about the grave clothes?

20:8   Who went in to the tomb next?

20:9   What did they not understand yet?

20:10   Where did the disciples go?

20:11   What did Mary do?

20:12   What did she see?

20:13   What did they ask her?
What did she say?

20:14   When she turned around, whom did she see?
Did she recognize Him?

20:15   What did He say to her?
What was she thinking?

20:16   What did Jesus say that made her recognize Him?
What did Mary call Him?

20:17   What did He tell her to do?
What was she to tell them?

20:18   Mary went and told them what?

20:19   Where were the disciples?
Why was the door locked?
What happened?

20:20   What did He show them?
What was their emotion?

20:21   What did He tell them?

20:22   What did He do to them?
What did they receive?

Notes on Prophecy:

There are hundreds of Messianic prophecies, which Jesus Christ fulfilled. Twenty-nine of these Old Testament prophecies were fulfilled within the 24 hours from His betrayal to His death. These prophecies are listed below:

Prophecy	Old Testament (prophecy)	New Testament (fulfilled)
Betrayed by a friend	*Psalm 41:9*	*Matthew 10:4*
Sold for 30 pieces of silver	*Zechariah 11:12*	*Matthew 26:15*
Money thrown in God's house	*Zechariah 11:13*	*Matthew 27:5*
Price given for potter's field	*Zechariah 11:13*	*Matthew 27:7*
Forsaken by His disciples	*Zechariah 13:7*	*Mark 14:50*
Accused by false witnesses	*Psalm 35:11*	*Matthew 26:59-61*
Remained silent before accusers	*Isaiah 53:7*	*Matthew 27:12-19*
Wounded and bruised	*Isaiah 53:5*	*Matthew 27:26*
Smitten and spit upon	*Isaiah 50:6*	*Matthew 26:67*
Mocked	*Psalm 22:7-8*	*Matthew 27:31*
Fell under the cross	*Psalm 109:24, 25*	*John 19:17; Luke 23:26*
Pierced	*Psalm 22;16*	*Luke 23:33*
Crucified with thieves	*Isaiah 53:12*	*Matthew 27:38*
Interceded for His persecutors	*Isaiah 53:12*	*Luke 23:34*
Rejected by His own people	*Isaiah 53:3*	*John 7:5, 48*
Hated without a cause	*Psalm 69:4*	*John 15:25*
Viewed from afar off	*Psalm 38:11*	*Luke 23:49*
People shook their heads at Him	*Psalm 109:25*	*Matthew 27:39*
Stared upon	*Psalm 22:17*	*Luke 23:35*
Garments parted and lots cast	*Psalm 22:18*	*John 19:23, 24*
Suffered thirst	*Psalm 69:21*	*John 19:28*
Offered gall and vinegar	*Psalm 69:21*	*Matthew 27:34*
Cried out	*Psalm 22:1*	*Matthew 27:46*
Committed Himself to God	*Psalm 31:5*	*Luke 23:46*
Unbroken bones	*Psalm 34:20*	*John 19:33*
Broken heart	*Psalm 22:14*	*John 19:34*
Pierced side	*Zechariah 12:10*	*John 19:34*

Darkened land	*Amos 8:9*	*Matthew 27:45*
Buried in rich man's tomb	*Isaiah 53:9*	*Matthew 27:57-60*

20:23   What were they permitted to do?

20:24   Who was not with them?

20:25   What did Thomas say he had to do before he would believe?

20:26   One week later, what happened?

20:27   What did He tell Thomas to do?

20:28   What did Thomas say?

20:29   What people will be blessed?

20:30   What did Jesus do?

20:31   Why were these things written for us?
         What would believing bring?

Application

1.   What did I learn about our God from this chapter?

2.   Was there a promise for me?

3.   Was there a command for me to obey?

4.   How should this affect my life today?

5.   Summarize this chapter.

John 21

Topics:
Jesus' Appearance
Peter Restored
Victory Complete

21:1   Where did He appear to His disciples next?

21:2   Name the disciples that were together.

21:3   Who said, "I'm going fishing"?
         What did they catch?

21:4   Early in the morning, who stood on shore?
         What did the disciples not realize?

21:5   What did Jesus ask?
         What was their answer?

21:6   What did He tell them and what happened?

21:7   Who told Peter it was the Lord?
         What did Peter do?

21:8   Who followed?
         How far from shore where they?

21:9   What did they see when they got to shore?

21:10   What did Jesus say?

21:11   How many large fish were there?

21:12   What did the disciples know?

21:13   What did He give to them?

21:14   How many times had Jesus been seen by the disciples?

21:15   What did Jesus ask Simon?
          What was Peter's answer?
          What did He tell him to do?

21:16   The second time, what did He ask him?
          What did Jesus command?

21:17   The third time, what did Jesus ask?
          What did this do to Simon?
          What was Peter's response?
          What was Jesus' command?

21:18   What did Jesus say would happen to Peter?

21:19   Why did Jesus say this?
          What did He command Peter?

21:20   Whom did Peter turn to and see?

21:21   What did Peter ask?

21:22   What was our Lord's response?

21:23   What rumor was spread?

21:24   *Note: John wrote this and yet he never used his name.*

21:25   Was everything that Jesus did written down?
          Why not?

Note: *If we had everything recorded that Jesus did, we could not carry the books. We just have what we need now until He comes for us.*

Application

1.   What did I learn about our God from this chapter?

2.   Was there a promise for me?

3.   Was there a command for me to obey?

4.   How should this affect my life today?

5.   Summarize this chapter.